ONE THOUSAND YELLOW BUTTERFLIES

poems by

KRYSTAL GRANT

ONE THOUSAND YELLOW BUTTERFLIES

poems by

KRYSTAL GRANT

KENELY
BOOKS

BOOKS BY KRYSTAL GRANT

Under the Palmetto Tree: A Novella
The Miseducation of Ms. G
Brooklyn
Poppy and the Play Date
Poppy's Pet Adventure

One Thousand Yellow Butterflies
Krystal Grant

F I R S T   E D I T I O N

ISBN: 978-1-954332-10-2

Cover Photo ©NexTser

Published by Kenely Books,
An Imprint of Wyatt-MacKenzie

For my mother,
Okla Chatman Kenely

That place
halfway between sleep and awake
is where I search for you

Table of Contents

I. HOME

II. SKY

III. LOVE

HOME

UNDER THE PALMETTO TREE

Pollen falls like a quiet rainstorm
A little girl sits under a palmetto tree
watching beads of yellow dust
drip on her silky brown skin

Her thick hair is loosely gathered in a puff
at the top of her head
It's the best her father could do
with the time he was given

She wipes the crust from her eyes
and cleans the dirt from her fingernails
Her dress is decorated with grass stains
from the day before

Cocoa butter greases her face
She is beautiful
The girl looks up to Heaven
and her spirit leaps with thoughts of her mother

She squints her eyes
and shields her face from the sun
Glaring into the sky
she searches for a sign

Momma, are you there?
Can you see me?
Her eyes grow wide with anticipation
and a smile decorates her face

The girl watches as her mother
descends from a cloud
like a feather that
got away from a fleeing bird

She has come

The mother takes the child into her arms
without saying a word
She carries the girl down a hill to flowing water
and carefully undresses the child

She bathes her daughter in the cool of the Santee River
as the girl rubs her wet hands across her mother's face
She dries the child's clean body and
gives her a beautiful white dress to wear

They sit on the bank of the Santee
while the mother gently brushes her daughter's hair
She twists the thick black coils
and allows them to hang to the girl's shoulders

She kisses the child on the cheek and
watches as the girl
skips away through the grass-
her hair bouncing on her back

The girl turns and her eyes follow
her mother as she ascends into the clouds
The child is at peace knowing she will meet her mother
again under the palmetto tree

COTTON FIELDS

I ain't neva seen no jasmine flower
But I seen cotton
Circled puff balls attached to a spiny stem
bouncing across a field bending themselves
to my ancestor's weary hands
waiting to be pulled and plucked

The thorns tear against my momma's fingers
and she winces in pain
careful not to draw the ire of the overseer
who squints fiercely in her direction

She bends her back deeper to the ground
and wipes sweat from her brow
She fills her bag with the white puff balls
and dreams of clear blue water

SWAN LAKE

Poetry awaits me
like an expectant mistress
searching for her nighttime love

She hears the hum of his engine
below her window pane
and readies herself for the magic
he will display under her sheets

Poetry is my love

It cleanses my mind
like a spring rain shower
dancing over ponds
of crooked-necked swans

I can't sleep
The thought of you
vexes my soul and
clenches my heart

I cannot breathe
I cannot breathe without you

SHE'S GONE

I heard my momma's voice today
It whispered in the wind

The melody from her lips
sent a chill through me

I reached out to touch her arm
but she hid from my embrace

Momma laughed as I searched for her

I turned around and around
peering through palmetto trees

gazing behind the crescent moon
looking beneath jessamine flowers

Her spirit returned to Heaven
before I could say goodbye

THE DEVIL ON A DIRT ROAD

The devil sat on the side of a winding dirt road
waiting for me to pass
His spine protruded from the arch in his back
A cloud of dust surrounded him as gnats encircled his
    head
and frogs bounced at his feet

The grass beneath him withered and died
turning a dark brown shade
succumbing to his evil stench
He smelled of bodily waste
His eyes seeped mud

As I approached, he stood and glared at my face
Rubbing his coal-stained hands together his smiled
The devil glided towards me and blocked my path
Clearly, he expected me to turn and run
But my feet had firmly planted themselves on the lonely
    dirt road

I did not move

There was a light that emerged from my spirit
and permeated through every part of my soul
It traveled down to my feet and out to my fingers
My mind was filled with a blanket of peace
and my heartbeat slowed

I inhaled the sweet smell of jessamine
and saw a lamb grazing in the distance
My mother hovered above us
She was joined by 1,000 friends all wearing white robes
with gold tassels

The devil stretched his neck to look above
Veins protruded from his throat
I watched as earthworms crawled from his nose
The grazing lamb drew closer to us
causing the devil to fall to the ground.

Blinded by the light, he raised his arm to shield his eyes
He screamed in pain as crud spewed from his ears
The earth shook then opened with a resounding rumble
The devil sunk into the deep crater that formed below
    him
The earth was restored

A jessamine flower bloomed at my feet
and a rainbow formed in the sky
My momma and her thousand friends disappeared in a
    cloud
I continued my path while the lamb, still grazing stayed
    by my side.

MY SPIRIT IS VEXED

My spirit is vexed with the thought of Heaven
Clear blue skies with light shining from the throne
     of God

Angels singing with hands lifted in praise
Hallelujah! Hallelujah!

My momma sitting quietly at the gate rocking back and
forth
thinking about her daughters

Sneaking away ever so often to visit them in their dreams
Hey Krystal, I'm OK. I'm OK.

A SINNER'S PRAYER

Hold my hand and rock me to sleep
Tell me everything will be fine

A glass of warm milk may have worked in the past
but it simply won't do this time

You see, I've stumbled along into some mess
and can't quite get myself out

My emotions are tied up in this sin
and honestly, I'm beginning to doubt

Are you real, Lord, or a really intricate
made-up fictional take

The Bible is nice, I read the whole thing
But parts of it are really quite pale

That wall that exists between you and I
I wish I could tear it all down

There's a hole in my heart growing large and wide
it's causing me to drown

I'm fighting for air. I want to be free
but this sin has locked me up tight

walking through darkness down a scary path
I'm desperately searching for light

I can't even finish this poem 'cause
I'm blinded. I really can't see

I'm struggling dear God, so if you are real
will you rescue a sinner like me?

I remember my mom in church singing hymns
with her hands lifted up to the sky

I didn't know then but I certainly do now
know the reason she would cry

I'm praying to you for a release from this
There seems to be no way out

This thing is so wrong. But it feels so good
Please, God, what is this about?

Save me, Lord. Set me free
from these awful, burdensome chains

This sin that I'm in is causing me grief
and leaving my spirit in pain

If it were up to me I'd stay right here
involved in this torrid space

As I said before, it feels so good
But my spirit is out of place

Cleanse me, Lord. Pull me up.
Rock me in your loving arms

Shower me in your mighty Word
and keep me from all harm

I lift my hands and now I cry
like my mother did before

Take me, Lord, for I am yours
A sinner I'll be no more

WHEN I CAN'T SLEEP

Carolina pities me in the springtime
with its bright yellow buds
of jasmine swinging in the breeze

I lift my sorrowed, sullen head
and look off into the distance
"There go them flowers waving at me"

A smile surprises my face
makes my eyes turn into skinny black lines
as my cheeks emerge from a frown

NIGHT DREAMS

In the middle of the night there is a knocking at my soul
It's my momma requesting entrance into my dreams

I gladly open the door and let her in
widening my arms, giving her soft body a place to fall.

She walks past and sits in a corner chair
Momma never did like hugs

She doesn't say much in my dreams-
just sits quietly watching, wishing, hoping

Hoping that we're OK - that she didn't leave us too soon.
We're OK, momma. We're OK.

`

EASTERN TIGER SWALLOWTAIL

I whispered your name
into the wind

You came back
and I could fly

I stood with my eyes closed
arms open
hoping for you to return

Birds fluttered about
watching curiously

A yellow butterfly
perched on my nose

It told me you were there
by the river succumb with grief

GREELEYVILLE HIGHWAY

Greeleyville Highway is a long, lonely trek
Fields and fields of tobacco line the road
As I walk along the pavement
my destiny is being fulfilled
With each step homeward
cotton bounces in the wind
waving its white puffs
toward my path

An old Ford pick-up
sits singularly in a yard
Rust decorates it on all sides

making it melancholy

A silver windmill twirls
It's blades spin in circles
powered by the breath
of enslaved people

stuck in a field of crops

It's time to go home
My mother stands in the kitchen
with an apron tied around her waist
and a rag covering her head
She lifts her hand to her side
and it settles on her large hips
She stirs a pot of black eyed peas
The heat rises to her face
and she blows the steam away

I stand on a wooden porch
watching her through the screen door

She moves round the kitchen with ease
despite her large size
I can see the weight of the world on her back
as she prepares dinner for her girls
Her life is not what she intended it to be
But she has settled on what it is
and makes the best of it

She does little to hide her frustration
with the pan of burnt macaroni
My mother pulls it from the oven
and scrapes the black crust from the top
This is not the dinner she intended it to be
But she has settled on what it is
and makes the best of it

With a shaky voice
I call out to the woman standing over the stove
She pays me no mind
and continues preparing dinner
I call out again
and my voice falls to the floor
before reaching my mother
Taking one last look at the large woman
I pin my head against the screen door
realizing no conversation will ever be had again

FIVE SISTERS

Five sisters sat in a hospital chapel
not knowing what to make of their new lives
Each of them recognized the violent shift
that had fallen upon them
but had simply allowed the weight of change
to be put aside until a more suitable time

They sat in chairs with distance between them
their purses dispersed haphazardly on the floor
Their speech was lazy, but their bodies were tense
and their breathing heavy
They spoke with heads bowed
afraid to look one another in the eye

Thinking of their father
who was left alone to say his final goodbyes
to his newly departed wife
the sisters talked of tasks that needed to be done that day
and quickly made a plan, in anticipation of the throngs
of visitors they would soon have to greet

Their mother was dead
And so, their spirits had died with her
What was to become of their lives?
No one was sure
But there was no life, no true life
without their mother

With scarves tied around their heads-
a signal of the 5:00 morning call they received from
    the hospital
they shifted their bodies nervously across the chairs
An eerie silence fell upon them as they contemplated
their morning. "We did everything we could," a male

nurse stated
in a solemn voice, "but were unable to save her."

A soft, baby blue blanket was spread taut
across their mother's body
All breathing apparatuses and life-support machines
were placed neatly above her bed
The tips of their mother's fingers had already

begun to turn a dark purple
"I am free. Thank the Lord I'm free.
No longer bound. No more chains
holding me. My soul is resting. And it's a blessing.
Thank the Lord. Hallelujah I'm free."
The oldest sister's shaky
voice managed to push out the song
causing everyone to sob

Their father sat in a corner with his head
nestled on the top of his walking cane
A scripture was read from a ragged Bible
The youngest sister locked eyes on her sibling
And sauntered around her mother's bed
Resting her head on her sister's shoulder

This was a day they would not soon forget;
the worst day they'd ever experience
Their minds churned with worry, their spirits
succumbed to anxiety, their hearts broken
Each of them, sitting separately in the chapel
but having one collective thought...

What next?

SKY

CLOUDS

I heard my momma's voice today
It was singing through the clouds
whispering with the wind

I squinted my eyes to catch a glimpse of her
Hands stretched wide to have her love
rain down upon me

With eyes closed
my body was overtaken with her love
enrapturing my imagination

My feet lifted off the ground
I took flight and joined her
in the clouds

CLOUDS OVER CAROLINA

Overwhelmed by the world
and drowning in pain
I look to the clouds
Bright puff balls
swimming in an ocean of blue
dancing in bright sunrays
rolling with the wind

Palmetto trees hover
just above my head
supplying me with shade
from grief

An orb of night strangely
glows in the sky
The crescent moon
illuminating my face
following my path

Downtrodden, I walk towards
Heaven in search of my mother
God's glory surrounds me
igniting every inch of my soul
I find peace with the Lord

He gently strokes my tear-soaked face
and warms my heart
I bow down in worship
Hallelujah! Glory!

MY MOTHER IS THERE

My mother is there
beyond the outstretched trees
she stands as a statue
with the golden sun bouncing on her back

My mother is there
amid the blades of grass
that reach to her waist
and sway in the cool breeze of spring

My mother is there
down by a stream
of blue flowing water
that trickles gently into the lake

My mother is there
Can't you see her form?
Her full lips and soft cheeks
That gather into a heap when she smiles

My mother is there
Can't you see her shadow?
Her tufts of jet black hair
that bend like waves upon her head

She calls out to me
but I cannot answer
Tears well into my eyes as
she beckons for my reply

ARTISTRY

My very first volume of poetry
will be written solely for you
One hundred magnificent love songs
One hundred pages of truth

Oh! How your artistry touched me
My! How my heart does leap
Incredible is your beauty
My love for you runs deep

LIGHTNING

With a flash of lightning
that lit up the night's sky
God answered my prayer

I stood singularly
wearing a purple shirt
 tattered by bleach spots
arms folded across my chest

listening to the eerie silence
afraid of the darkness that enveloped me
I pleaded with the Almighty
"I need your help, God."

In an instant the sky was illuminated
making visible the heavy clouds
that hung from the stars

God had heard me
He had answered my prayers
I looked up to Heaven
in hopes of seeing His face
Another flash of light- softer, quicker

In that moment my chest swelled with warmth
And my mind welcomed the presence of the Lord
He hears my voice.

RAINBOW

In the distance
a rainbow tickles my eye
It is perfectly arched
with colors pouring from the sky
The spectrum is distinct
and bright

Raindrops still wet the air
leaving dense clouds of moisture
hanging just above the ground
Soft rumbles of thunder
shake my soul
And a few flashes of light
are left behind

The storm has gone
leaving a perfect arch
as a promise of peace
I close my eyes
Sun rays slowly break through
the clouds and shine on my face
I am loved

THE DARK OF NIGHT

I dreamt of death
It crept upon me
like a heavy mist that sits
upon a swamp
in the dark of night

I did not allow his sadness
to overtake my soul
I smiled
and greeted him kindly
tipping my hat towards his horror

Turning my back to his filth
I walked away
with boldness
knowing God would not
allow him to follow

I am covered

PANDEMIC

We are hibernating
like bears in the winter
little contact with the outside world
Slowed breathing
Peaceful
Calm
A beautiful distraction from our everyday trials
We are hibernating

YELLOW BUTTERFLY

A yellow butterfly dances in front of me
I squint my eyes to shield myself from the morning sun
and fan it away with my hand

With the afternoon heat beating against my back
a yellow butterfly flutters around my head
making me dizzy

In the cool of the Carolina evening
a yellow butterfly perches itself on my knee
and waves in my direction

Hello, mother. I've missed you too.

ONE THOUSAND YELLOW BUTTERFLIES

One thousand yellow butterflies
surrounded my soul
and I took flight
above the trees
into the clouds

But I didn't quite make it into Heaven
My mother stood at the gates, engulfed in an incredible light
She smiled and giving me a stern look,
waved her finger
disapprovingly.

"No, Krystal. It's not time. You have more to do.
Much more.
Go back and be great."

I drifted back to earth
with 1,000 yellow butterflies
fluttering around me.

They led me to the path that I should walk.
Encircling my body,
the butterflies guided me along a dirt road
towards Greeleyville.
With each step a small cloud of dust formed around my worn
feet.

I grew weary as the South Carolina sun
beat against my back.
The yellow butterflies shielded me
from its stinging rays.

I wiped beads of sweat from my forehead
and looked up to heaven.

Momma was watching me, smiling.

The butterflies' wings flickered
in front and behind me.
I could not see my path.
But I felt the cool breeze of their wings
blowing on my face.

LOVE

SOFT LANDINGS

Underneath this hard exterior
of frustration
indifference
profanity
toughness
I need you to know that I am still
a woman
Soft
Loving
Kind-hearted

I like flowers
candy
little boxes wrapped in bows
strong hugs
easy conversations
strokes on my arm
and a soft place to land

LOVE
(for Nikki Giovanni)

I am not supposed to love you
I can't control myself

I have trouble falling asleep
because my mind spins with thoughts of you

And when I manage to slumber
I dream of your kisses

As the sun comes up and I awake
a smile lights my face because you are there
in my thoughts

I feel you when you are miles away
I search the air for your scent
I am consumed

I am not supposed to love you
but I do

I

I am having trouble focusing
I can't get you out of my mind
I inhale breaths of you
I have no concept of time

I adore the sound of your voice
I cling to the stroke of your touch
I burn with desire for you
I admit, it can be too much

I need to feel you near me
I listen for the beat of your heart
I bathe in all your glory
I loved you from the start

I smile when you enter a room
I dance towards your embrace
I delight in your every move
I am in awe of your beautiful grace

I won't let this feeling go
I will stay forever with you
I dedicate my life and soul
I swear that I'll be true

HAMPTON, VIRGINIA

The house is a little more empty
The rooms are a little less warm
The air is a little less noisy
Now that you are gone

Your bedroom remains in tact
Just as you left it last
Clothes strewn here and there
Dust sprinkled on the glass

I await your call each night
Think of you every day
Dream of your bright smile
And I often sit and pray

That God will lift my spirit
And ease my mind's distress
Bind our hearts together
And give our souls rest

IF
(for Rudyard Kipling)

If I am not the woman
you need me to be
then what woman is good enough?

If I let my hair grow long-
past the small of my back
will you love me then?

If I sashay around town
letting my hips swing wildly
this way and that
will it grab your attention?

If I let you make love to me at midnight
on the sandy shore of the Atlantic
will that satisfy your curiosity?

If I become stoic, pretending not to care,
instead of being this ball of emotional wreckage
will I be exactly what you need?

If my smile is not white enough
If my eyes are not bright enough
If my soul, too open and my heart
too dedicated for you to love me then
who, my darling? Who is enough?

LOVE SKY

I wrote a poem about you
but the foul odor of your memory
turned my stomach
and caused me to vomit

I tore the poem into tiny pieces
and scattered them around my room
My thoughts sprinkled the carpet
as stars sprinkle the night sky

There was a time
we soared upon clouds
and thought of nothing but love
Our minds submerged into ecstasy
Our hearts beating in unison

Then you pricked my soul
and I began to bleed
leaving a pool of hurt
dripping from our love sky

What have I done to you, my love?

LET ME

Let me just lay here and think of you
The way you make me feel
The warmth that enters my heart
This love I know is real

Let me just sit and imagine you
The smile that brightens my day
Your eyes that seem so stuck on me
In the very best of ways

Let me just stop and remember you
The smell of your cologne
Your fingers that tickle my side
I know I'm not alone

Let me just stand and reach out to you
Caress the back of your neck
Brown skin that I adore
My emotion are left unchecked

Let me just walk beside you
Secure in your embrace
Confident in your love
This feeling cannot be erased

UNWANTED

I will buy myself a dozen roses
and pretend they come from you

Create a neatly written card
and end it with "Love, forever"

I will lie to myself daily about your faithfulness
and dream of our evening walks

I will return to our bed, leaving space for you
and search for the memory of your breath
I will listen for your key to turn the door
and run to your arms as you enter

I will wait at the edge of hope for you
I will climb to the apex of anticipation
I will swim across galaxies for your touch
I will crumble into a million pieces
of unwanted love if you do not appear

Come to me, my love

A MEETING WITH DEATH

The rank scent of death
met me before daylight on June 12
The cool air of morning stung my cheek
as I rushed toward its darkness

Oh! How I despised him
as he stared me in the face
making a mockery of my pain

The world became silent
as death pulled all that I know
away from me

My heart sank deeper
into my chest as I tried to breathe

There was no air
my lungs filled with bile that
emerged from my gut

I was left alone
Completely alone
The sun began to rise
in the midst of my turmoil
But all that was before me
seemed dark, damp, dead

I pleaded with death
in the morning light
I begged to be taken instead
Take me
Take me

He was gone
And you, mother,
were nowhere to be found

I WANT TO WALK WITH YOU

I want to walk with you-
holding hands as we saunter
through the parking lot
making our way to the grocery store

Slowing my gait to match yours
Feeling your flesh against mine
Loving you - as your child – yet, your protector

I could not heal you
And I cannot heal this pain in my heart
This crushing of my soul that leaves me
spinning in a whirlpool

SOMETHING LIKE LOVE

You were a little too dismissive
on your way to work
The door slammed shut just after
mumbling a disingenuous "I love you"

My head hung low
as I turned toward the kitchen
to clean the breakfast you left behind
The house is silent. Lonely. Empty.

I try to sing a song
but the melody gets stuck on my tongue
so I settle for a soft hum
My heart is silent. Lonely. Empty.

Your words have little meaning
There was a time I hung on your every syllable-
every breath
Now, I can't stand to hear you breathe

I toss the uneaten meal into the trash
and clean the dish
A yellow butterfly flutters its wings
outside my kitchen window

My mind looks to the clouds
I am lifted toward the Heavens
by a cool burst of wind
Goodbye, my love.

IN THE BEGINNING

In the beginning was the word
A harsh, violent blow to my ego

that made me realize
you don't love me

So where am I to go now?
What am I to do with this pain?

My life begins and ends with you

I look around at the leaves
that have fallen from the trees

They engulf my feet and will not
allow me to move forward

I am stuck

I SEARCHED FOR A POEM

I searched for a poem about you
but decided to write one myself
No other writer could describe
the emotions my heart felt

the day I saw you standing there
with a longing in your eye
You looked into my soul
Now I can't say goodbye

Stay with me tonight
Hold me and don't let go
Let me rest there in your arms
This feeling I cannot control

COUNTDOWN
(with a nod to Kendrick Lamar)

Ten songs I sang for you
in the garden outside your home

Nine daffodil petals
I picked as I began to roam

Eight candles I sent to you
by mail to your address

Seven dreams I had of you
imagining your caress

Six incredible paintings I created
with the stroke of a brush

Five kisses I gave you
yet, you didn't even blush

Four times I called out to you
in hopes you'd hear my plea

Three long hours I waited
but you never answered me

Two daggers I used
to stab you in the heart

One casket to bury you
You should have loved me from the start

RETURN TO STARK STREET

An easy wind shifts rustic leaves
across the lawn
Blades of grass bend mercilessly
toward the ground
The florets of a dandelion
break away and drift toward my feet

I take a step forward
and hear a soft crunch
Looking down, I see an ant
crawling across the top of my shoe
carrying a grain of food
back to its nest

There's a bright cloud hanging
from the sky
beckoning my attention
I dare not look
For fear of seeing my mother's face
makes me tremble

It's been five years
since you've gone
Leaving me motherless
The world is cold and damp
without you
I am lost

This house is hallowed ground
Your books still line the shelves
Your clothes still hang in the closet
Your slippers, right where you left them
Nothing has been touched
For fear that your memory will disappear

MORNING
(for Darryl Pinckney)

Everything in this room has too much meaning
A bathrobe is thrown across the bedpost
Lint decorating its sleeves

The smell of you
touches my nose
as I place my feet in your bedroom slippers

An earthquake shook my entire soul today
Early, before the sun came up
Before I wiped the sleep from my eyes

The aftershock still resounds in me
I am spinning uncontrollably
deeper and deeper into a black hole

Above my head dust has accumulated
The ceiling fan is lined with specks of gray
and spider webs hang in a corner

There is too much to move
too much to think about
too much to feel

Our late afternoon calls have ended
Your voice is now a memory
and the pain is crushing

I pull my feet from your slippers
and stand in the midst of your aura
You smell of yellow jessamine

I inhale
and listen as my lungs
take in your air

I can hear the hustle
of a vacuum cleaner
hurriedly rolling over carpet

But my heart is silent
The stillness of this room
tears me in two
This morning
you left me
And I am gone with you

OVERCOME

There's a queen buried deep in inside me
that you have brought to light

She was wrapped in peasant clothing
depressed and walking through night

Her head hung low, sunken eyes
Tears crowning under her chin

Broken and bruised, tattered and torn
Such darkness outside and in

Then you came along with your gentle soul
and peeled away the worn down parts

You kissed every tear, made everything right
fixed every inch of this heart

So hear I am, an open field
of jasmine flowers dancing in sun

You've touched my heart and given me life
I admit, I'm overcome

A queen in all her glory
Yet, hopelessly yearning for you

I am yours, my love. Totally consumed
Tell me what you want me to do

ONE LOVE
(for Kwame Dawes)

My fingers float across the books
that line my shelf
They have been here for years-
colorful, salient reminders
of my love affair with words

It is only because of you that I know
Walcott, Braithwaite, Goodison
You love them deeply
You made me love them

Nearly twenty years have past
But I remember as if it were yesterday

Your scraggly beard covering your face
Leather sandals exposing your rough, worn feet
And a button shirt hiding your protruding belly

You should take better care of yourself
Eat healthier, comb your hair
Attend to your body as much as you attend to your mind

Buchi Emicheta stares at me from the shelf
I remember how quickly I read her book
I wanted to lead the class discussion with vigor-
make you proud

I must have said something meaningful
You looked at me through your broad spectacles
and said "well done" in your heavy Jamaican accent

All of your autographs read the same
Blue ink, forceful, hasty writing:

"For Krystal, One love. Kwame"

I remember you well and think of you fondly

I stroke my hand across Colin Channer, Danticat
Gordimer, Awooner, Lovelace
I should read these books again soon
My memory of the characters has faded

But my memory of you holds strong

AND STILL

I've circled the sun
a thousand times
and still cannot find you

I gave you my heart
my body and mind
and still my words are true

Come back to me, dear
My arms are out-stretched
Here. Forever I'll wait

To see you again
is all that I ask
Now. Do not hesitate

I swam the ocean,
climbed every hill
and still you ignore my plea

Time will not stop
My love will not change
And still you won't come to me

There is nothing left
but a broken heart
and a tattered, mangled soul

A helpless spirit
A downtrodden body
And a love left out in the cold

SUMTER, SOUTH CAROLINA

There's a flea market
on highway 76/378
just past Shaw Air Force Base
that my mother would take me to
on Saturdays

We would pass each vendor's booth slowly
I'd beg for all that was being sold
She wouldn't buy me much
but that didn't matter
because I was with her

Soft brown skin
Hair grazing the back of her neck
Fluffy cheeks and a perfect smile
She was wonderful

THE TROUBLE WITH WOMEN

The trouble with women is
we think too much
about things that don't require thought

We sway to the beautiful music of our souls
feeling totally alive and free
We get lost in the rhythm
throw our hands up in joy
welcoming the melody into our spirits

Then our minds take ahold of us
and we begin to wonder if our
bra straps are showing
Are our bellies bulging out
from under our skirts?

The music gets lost in the recesses of our
cluttered minds
The melody drips away from our spirits
We close the doors to our freedom
and we are lost forever

ON GOING NATURAL

Why do I care
your opinion of my hair?

Whether it be long or short
braids or bald
what you think
doesn't matter at all

If I shave the sides
or curl the back
It's up to me
I like it like that

Grow a mohawk or locs
dye it blonde or blue
I'm the same ol' Krystal
tried and true

And a silver nose ring
might suit me just fine
Four piercings in my ears
'lil profanity on the side

So wrinkle your nose
at someone else's style
I'm getting another tattoo
I'll be back in a while

WHY WON'T YOU COME?

Dreams invade my mind
I try to shake the thought of you but
 the weight of my grief
renders me incapable

Sadness sustains me now
I have no use of food, water, shelter
It's only my yearning for you that keeps me alive
Where are you?

Can you not feel the loneliness that envelops me?
Can you not see the hole in my heart?
Can you not taste the bitter air that I must breathe?
Life doesn't matter

Dreams invade my mind
I try to shake the thought of you but
the sour stench of living
has made me complacent

I am ravaged by darkness
I have no use of light, laughter, love
It's only my longing for you that keeps me awake
Why won't you come?

LEAD ME AWAY

One day I'll write something great
and the world will cheer

What is this overriding sense of
worthlessness that stays with me;

this feeling of not enough
that drives me to do more?

Yet sends me to the corner
to sulk in my paltry state?

I'm stagnant at times
listening to love songs
in hopes of rocking
the anguish away

I am numb

I'll contort my body in various forms
to hide the hole in my heart

The bleak, dark spaces in my spirit
that won't allow me to live

But you see through my
bends, my twists and contortions

You see the small flower that grows inside
starving for nutrients, yet surviving, flourishing

Take me away. Lead me out
of this affliction
Where I will be free
to soar unbounded by troubles

Lead me away

BADLY WRITTEN POEMS

I sent him a badly written poem
in hope that he would tell me he loved me

Instead he scoffed and added my poem
to a pile of trash littering a corner of his office

He hates me. He told me so many years ago
when I sat at his feet playing love songs on my guitar

He rubbed off my kisses with the back
of his hand and laughed at my tears

I died inside, but continued
strumming my guitar at his feet

I sent him a badly written poem
in hope that he would tell me to marry him

Instead he danced with the girl in the corner
and rubbed the inside of her thigh with his leg

He loves me. I know he does because he smiled
when I poured him a cup of coffee at the corner diner

He wiped his mouth with the back of his hand
and rubbed his chest with satisfaction

I laughed inside because the hair on his face
was littered with drops of brown liquid

I sent him a badly written poem
in hope that I could get him out of my mind

Instead he wrote me back asking if he could
walk with me along the beach at midnight

I hate him. He has wrung my heart and caused
me to cry myself to sleep every night.

I slit my wrist and watched as the blood
poured from my arm into the ocean

He wrapped my wrist in cloth to stop the bleeding
but I closed my eyes and died in his arms.

A SONG AT MIDNIGHT

I need to tell you I miss you
but figure you don't care

Sing you a song at midnight
in the cold winter air

Swim across an ocean
to have you close to me

Run a thousand marathons
to see you in my dreams

Scream your name in a stadium
of 80,000 fans

Caress your beautiful face
just to feel you in my hands

Write a silly love poem
that you will never read

Walk away in tears
since you won't fulfill my need

ONE MILLION

I can think of a million
gifts to buy you
Package them neatly in colorful boxes
with cute little bows
Place them strategically under my tree
and wait for the 25th of December
to give them to you
Watch as a smile lights your face
with every gift you unwrap

I can think of a million
kisses to place on your body
Lovingly caress your skin
as I drag my lips this way and that
Listen to you breathe as you
anticipate my next move
Shiver as your hand dandles my thigh

I can think of a million
ways to love you
but you are not mine
and I am not yours
You have ascended
into the Carolina clouds
and I am left alone
on a dirt road

HEARTBURN

I don't want to read any love poems
or hear any songs about you

Balloons and roses aren't suitable
Red hearts and candy won't do

I check my phone every minute
But text messages and calls are no more

I look out my peephole each hour
But have no letters or visits to my door

I inhale and accept the inevitable
I exhale and hope it's not true

My biggest fear has materialized
I guess I'm not good enough for you

I'm left on the side of the highway
Lost, not knowing where to turn

And all that is left to do
Is allow my poor heart to burn

BREATHE

I don't choose to care anymore
This feeling feels so free
Like a weight has lifted from my soul
and is allowing me to breathe

Letting go of foolish thoughts
and silly wants and dreams
Like a weight has lifted from my soul
and is allowing me to breathe

Being sick so long, my body is weak
but my spirit knows what I need
Like a weight has lifted from my soul
and is allowing me to breathe

It's not easy to walk away
cause I know just what this means
Like a weight had lifted from my soul
and is allowing me to breathe

I'll slowly turn and walk away
listening for your pleas
Like a weight has lifted from my soul
and is allowing me to breathe

You don't ask me to stay
or even get on your knees
Like a weight has lifted from my soul
and is allowing me to breathe

As a matter of fact you turned and ran
Disappearing in the trees
Like a weight has lifted from my soul
but it's hard for me to breathe

So now I stand and watch you go
hoping you'll return to me
Like a weight has descended on my soul
and now I cannot breathe

AILEY

I wish my life to be as beautiful as a dancer
Stretching across the stage with
magical leaps and soft pirouettes
Bowing before an audience
of appreciative onlookers
who marvel at my creativity and strength

Everyday an arabesque
Every night a plie
Every move a wonder
Every minute a joy

Let me stand before crowds
and show my handiwork
Create masterpieces
Causing tears to fall from their eyes
helping their hearts to heal

Let my life be as beautiful as a dancer

A MIGHTY WIND

She was a mighty wind
that caused a shift everywhere she went
Twisting trees
shaking rooftops
bending blades of grass

Now, she's a cool breeze
gliding through the clouds
Kissing my cheek as she
slides over my face to greet me

She was a clammy caterpillar
inside a rigid cocoon
with barely enough room to breathe
Locked in darkness

Now, she's a yellow butterfly
fluttering gently
across my path
as I make my way through this world

NEVER MIND

Never mind the heart shaped box of candy
Never mind the flowers and gifts
Never mind the poems
Never mind the love
Never mind our very first kiss

Never mind the way you grabbed my hand
and lead me through the world
Never mind the touch on the small of my back
Never mind making my toes curl

Never mind the way I said I love you
as you stroked the back of my neck
Never mind you coming into my life
Never mind our heart's intersect

Never mind the day you sent me flowers
Never mind the way I smile
Never mind the way we talked for hours
Never mind our walk down the aisle

Never mind me inhaling breathes of you
Never mind being totally consumed
Never mind the feelings I thought were true
Never mind, I shouldn't have assumed

THE DINNER TABLE
(for Strom Thurmond, et al.)

Sally Ann trudged to the dinner table
The swinging kitchen door pats her
on the behind giving her a swift nudge
as she enters the dining room.

She stares at the magnolia flowers
that line the porcelain platter
she carries between her hands.
Her eyes trace the emerald vines
that circle the dinnerware. She is careful not to look up.

The smell of ox tails and field peas line her nose.
Candles flicker from the corners of her eyes.
Her mind is consumed with setting the platter down
silently as not to arouse the wrath of Mrs. Thurmond
who glares at her in disgust.

The dish is placed on the table with ease.
Sally Ann knows full well what she should do-
turn and move towards the swinging
kitchen door to await further instructions.
But her eyes cannot help themselves.

They glance towards the head if the table
and catch the sight of him
looking back at her.
The corner of his mouth curls,
giving her an approving smile and quick nod.

Sally Ann's heart swells with joy
and she turns towards the kitchen door
to relish in the acknowledgement.
But her ears begin to burn as the screech
from Mrs. Thurmond rings through the room.

The woman slams her fork onto the fine china
scattering field peas across her plate.
She barks at the child for having threads hanging from her dress,
stating how lazy her mother must be
for having the child presented in such a way.

As she is scolded, Sally Ann thinks of her mother,
skin the color of obsidian, hips wide and strong,
neck narrow, eyes as beautiful as the moonlight-
much too generous and wise to be confined to a kitchen
subjected to the foolish whims of white people.

Sally Ann bows her head in obedience
and whispers a faint 'yes, ma'am'.

The hatred of the plantation
washes over Sally Ann-
eroding any joy she had received moments earlier.

Sally Ann looks down at her soft coconut skin
wondering how long it would be before Mrs. Thurmond
would strike her again
and how long Mr. Thurmond
would remain silent.

Remnants of a bruise still appear on
Sally Ann's forearm where Mrs. Thurmond
burned her with a candle.
Her mother had taken some fresh cow urine
and mixed it in a jar with Mrs. Thurmond's
lemonade as revenge.

Mrs. Thurmond drank the lemonade in slow,
easy gulps, asking her mother to pour another glass.

When Mrs. Thurmond shoos the child with her hand,
Sally Ann returns to the kitchen through the swinging door
with her long, wavy hair trailing behind.

MY MOTHER IS LIKE MAGIC

She can float on a cloud
through the South Carolina sky

She can sail on a lily pad
across the Santee River

She can rain on the tobacco fields of Greeleyville
and gather herself into puddles

My mother is like magic

She is my north star that has disappeared
leaving me lost in this wilderness

AN INCREDIBLE WOMAN
(for Madison)

You are such an incredible woman
I am in awe of you
The kindness of your spirit
the beauty of your soul
You are truly too good to be true

You are such an incredible woman
You run the race alone
Competing with no one
achieving your goals
Your power is unknown

You are such an incredible woman
My heart leaps for you
A precious gem
a shining star
The clearest of oceans blue

You are such an incredible woman
Your strength knows no bounds
Connected to God
walking in light
A joy to have around

You are such an incredible woman
Amazing and honest and true
The love of my life
my greatest work
A treasure through and through

A LETTER TO MY SONS
(for Collin and Chase)

God created you perfect
You are beautiful
You are wise, wonderful
There is an incredible purpose for your life
And you will thrive
You will grow
You will mature
you will excel

The light that shines upon you will brighten this world
because you are a problem solver
Within you are solutions to disease, corruption
pain and sorrow

Your soft brown skin glides across
my arm when you hug me
Your coily hair tickles my neck when
you bury your head in my chest
searching for comfort

Your big brown eyes have not
known pain because we have
comforted you, protected you
prayed for you

Because God saw fit
to bless you with such gifts
you will be hated. Despised
You will be underestimated
People will try hold you back
diminish your power

They will try to break your spirit

break your bones
But the light, that incredible light that
shines upon and within you cannot be dimmed
Your divine purpose will manifest
Your soul will shine through
Your strength will overpower evil
You will thrive
You will soar
You will transcend

TO MY MOTHER WHO IS NO LONGER HERE
(Mother's Day 2018)

There's an empty place
in the middle my heart.
That is where you should be

My soul has a stain
that can't be erased
It throbs uncontrollably

The breath I inhale
doesn't fill my lungs
because sorrow is resting inside

Sleepless nights
with long, painful days
and countless times I've cried

Your voice I can hear
in the back of my mind
And your touch I remember well

I creep through this life
with a crushed, angry spirit
but no one can truly tell

So, to my mother
who is no longer here
I think of you every day

I dream of you often
My head hangs somberly
with memories that won't go away

A PLEA TO THE MOST HIGH

Be the apology I never received
and the lesson I was never taught

Listen to my prayer as I'm on my knees
and put peace in my every thought

Be the healing of my painful scars
and joy washing over me

Be the stitching of my tattered soul
and the vision I need to see

Touch my ever restless flesh
Gift me with your grace

Cleans my stained, wretched mind
and put me into place

Mend the broken parts of me
and fill every empty hole

Cover all the exposed things
Raise me high when I am low

CPSIA information can be obtained
at www.ICGtesting.com
Printed in the USA
BVHW070437240321
603261BV00002B/131

9 781954 332102